Pierre the Pencil's Nature Journal

Writings and Drawings About His Uppercase Alphabet Adventure

Written and Illustrated by
Tori Lee, OTR/L, DrOT, ATP
Occupational Therapist

This Book Belongs To:

_____

Copyright © 2023 by Victoria Lee

All rights reserved. No part of this publication may be reproduced or transmitted in any form or by any means, electronic or mechanical, including photocopy, recording, or any information storage and retrieval system comma without permission in writing from the publisher.

IBSN 979-8-9899503-1-7 (paperback)
IBSN: 979-8-9899503-0-0 (ebook)

This book is dedicated to my Mom.
She is the reason I became an
occupational therapist.

Pierre the Pencil wants you to draw his letter pictures along with him while he shares his alphabet adventures through nature!

This book was written and illustrated by an occupational therapist. This book is intended to help students learn what capital letters look like by using things they see in nature. Pierre the Pencil also gives helpful tips and tricks along the way to help teachers teach the basics of letter formation and the directionality of letters. Drawing along with the book helps students to practice their uppercase letters, work on their fine motor and visual motor skills, and have fun while learning!

Thanks for supporting our students and their handwriting!

A great adventure always starts with mountains that stand tall like the letter A.

Bears are sometimes seen on adventures in the wilderness. I saw this bear on one of my hikes!

Days outside are sometimes filled with little green frogs hopping around rivers and lakes!

Every fun adventure has bridges that cross over rivers. It is nice when you can stand on top and watch the water flow below.

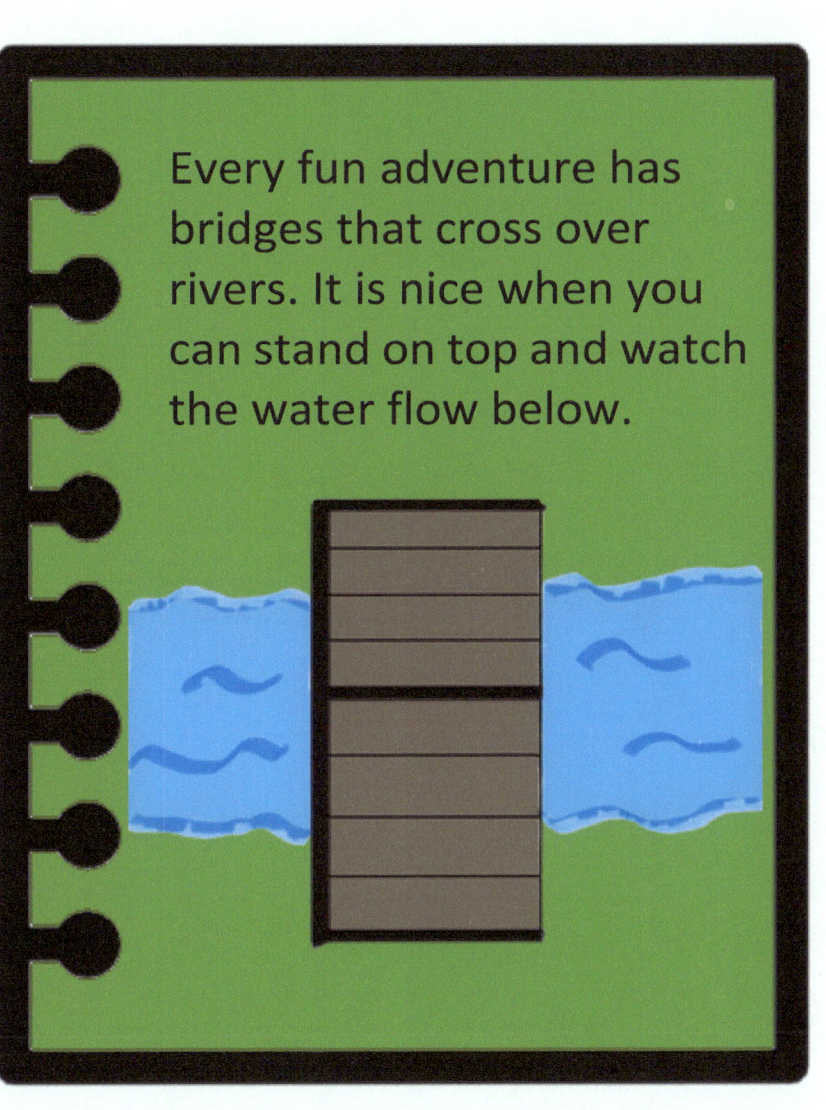

Falls are a beautiful sight to see while hiking! Water falls are all over the country. Have you seen one before?

Goats and big horn sheep climb high up in the mountains. They can be seen on rocky cliffs.

Icicles form along rooftops when it is cold and snowy outside. Water drips down them and freezes at the ends, making them longer and longer until they break off or melt away!

Just hanging around with my new caterpillar friend. James the caterpillar curls his head up to begin making his cocoon.

Keep away from skunks that spray! I don't want to be all stinky for the rest of my adventure!

Logs are seen all over nature. They can be fallen trees, homes for insects and animals, or can be used as firewood to keep us warm!

Mountains are tall and valleys are low. When you are adventuring it is always fun to hike up and down big mountains.

Never forget your tent when camping! It will keep you warm and dry if wind or rain comes. What a wonderful place to rest for the night!

Of course the sun is a very important part of nature! It gives plants and animals energy to live and grow!

People love to fish when they come across rivers and lakes. Look! Someone caught a fish!

Rock slide! Watch out! This was a scary day. But luckily I was alert and watching my surroundings when the rocks started to slide.

Sammy the Snake slithered right past me this morning. I was able to look at his yellow and green stripes right before he hid under a rock!

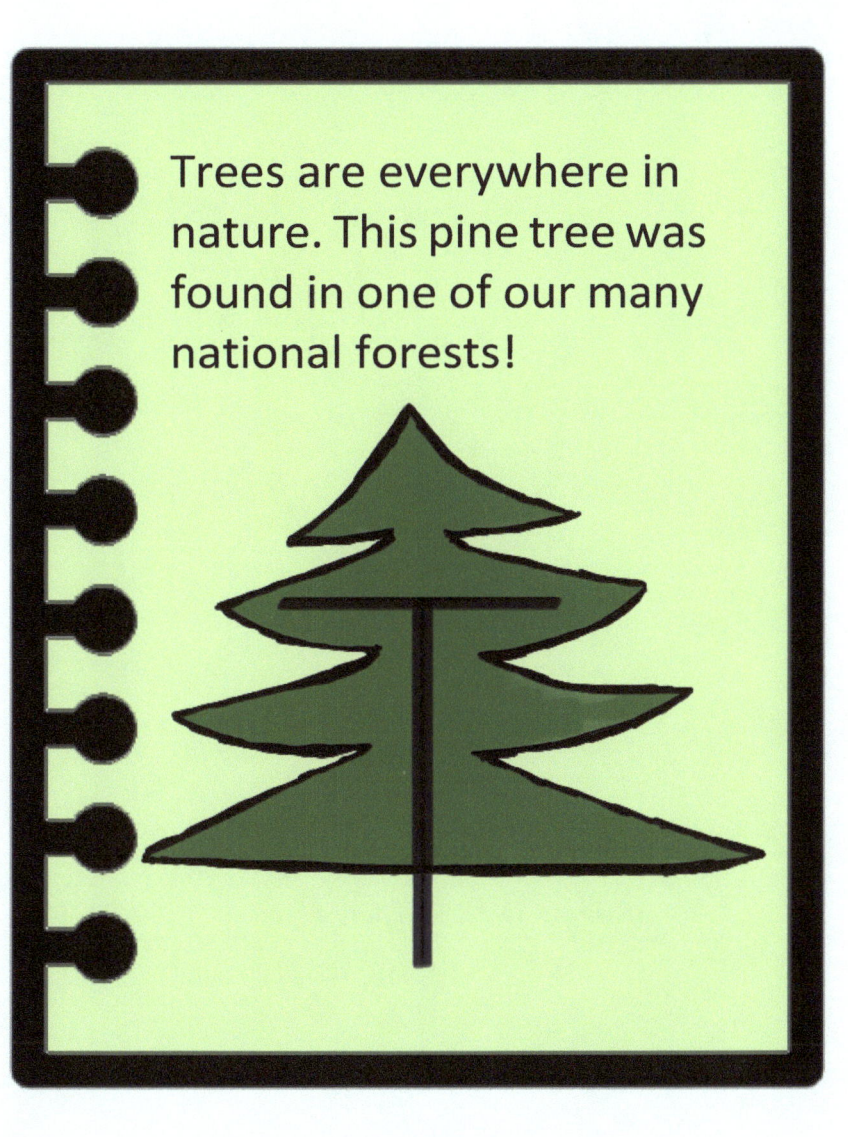
Trees are everywhere in nature. This pine tree was found in one of our many national forests!

Unpack your backpack full of supplies when you are done your adventure! This is the backpack that I brought along with me!

V formation is the pattern that birds, such as geese, fly in. This bird was shaped like a V, and so was his beak!

Willow bushes turn beautiful colors throughout the year. The ones I saw were a reddish, brown color.

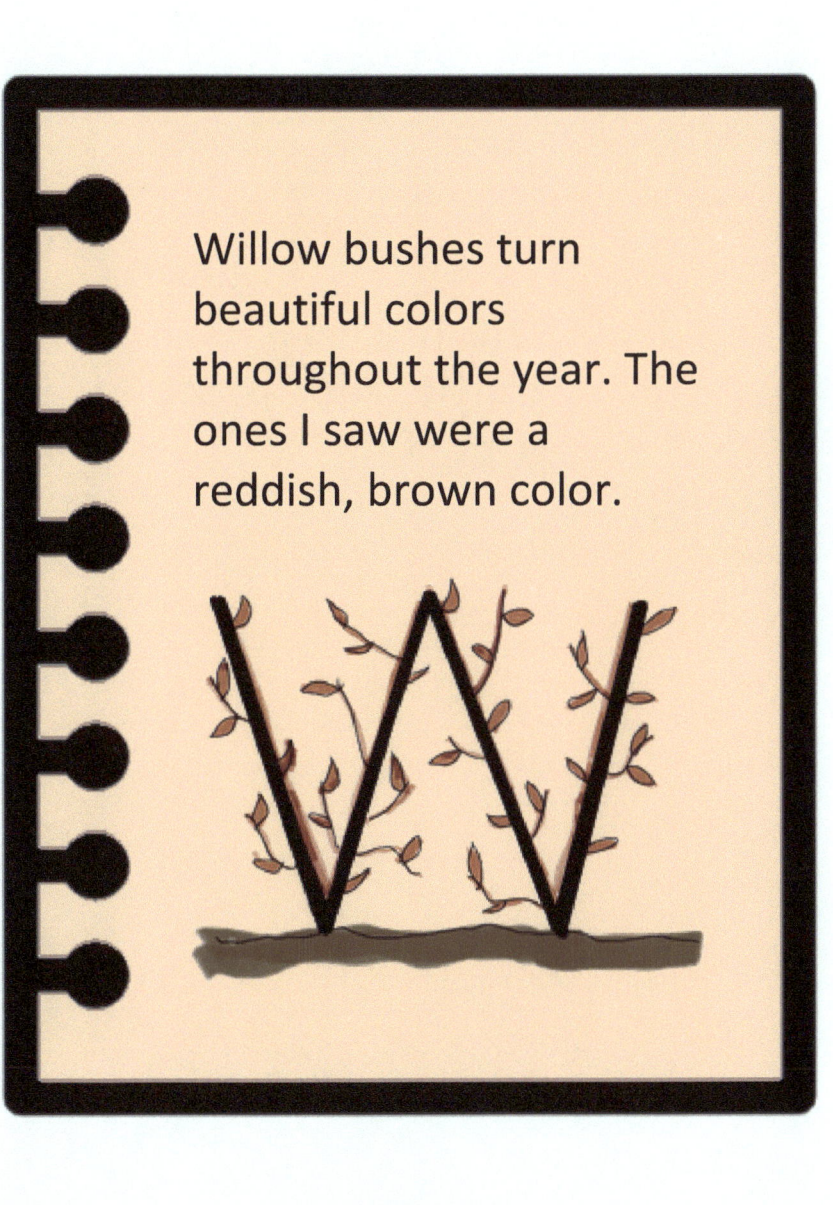

EXperiences like this are wonderful. Campfires are perfect for camp songs and s'mores!

You never know when you might come across something amazing on the ground! This antler, shed by a deer in the spring, was a fun find on this adventure!

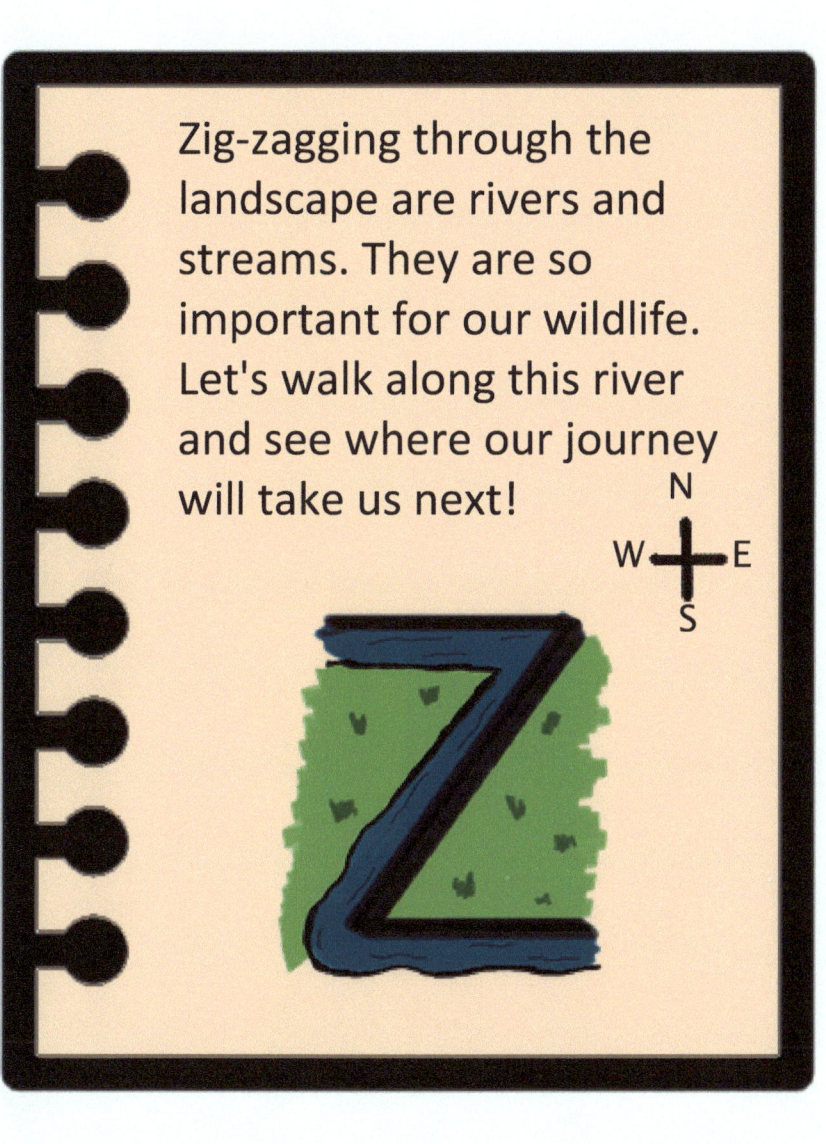

www.ingramcontent.com/pod-product-compliance
Lightning Source LLC
Chambersburg PA
CBHW041526090426
42736CB00035B/18